HOME

This book belongs to:

_ _

Victoria Plum

Victoria's Snowflake Net

Angela Rippon

PURNELL

SBN 361 05063 1

First published 1981 by Purnell Books, Paulton,
Bristol, BS18 5LQ, a member of the BPCC group.
Reprinted 1985.

Made and printed in Great Britain by Purnell and Sons
(Book Production) Limited, Paulton, Bristol.

All day in the Great Wood it rained, and rained, and rained. Not the gentle rain of spring, nor the boisterous showers that interrupt the warmth of a summer day, but the cold, hard, grey rain that says, "Winter is here."

Victoria Plum sat in front of the fire in her rambling old tree house and warmed her toes and fingers. Outside, the wind was tearing at the trees and the rain had turned the wood into a wet, soggy mess.

"Today is definitely a day for staying indoors," thought Victoria, as she snuggled down into her comfortable old bean bag with a cup of barley soup and a book. Victoria was so engrossed in the story that she did not notice the flames of the fire gradually dying. Suddenly she felt chilly. Where the flames had been dancing was now a pile of grey ash.

"Oh, silly me," muttered Victoria. "Now I shall have to lay the fire again." She set to work with paper and kindling, and in no time at all the sticks were crackling and the fire filled Victoria's room with a warm glow. The log basket in the corner was now almost empty.

"I had better fill that up," she thought to herself. "I don't want the fire to go out again." Victoria kept a store of logs outside her kitchen. When she opened the door, the house was filled with the sound of splattering rain and angry wind. As she piled the logs into the basket, Victoria thought she heard another noise above the roar of the storm.

V

"That wasn't the wind," she said, "or the rain." It was only a very faint noise, but it sounded to Victoria as if someone was crying out.

"Is anyone out there?" shouted Victoria.

"Yes. I'm over here," replied a very faint voice.

The rain was so heavy it was like a thick watery curtain and poor Victoria could hardly see a thing.

"Wait a minute," she called. "I'm coming," and she dashed indoors to pull on her raincoat and wellingtons. Victoria thought the sound had come from the bottom of the wall below her house. She began searching around but she could not find anything. Then she moved towards a pile of stones. As she moved closer, the noise grew louder.

"I'm over here," said the voice. Victoria decided that whoever needed help must be invisible, because although she could hear them clearly, she still could not see anyone.

"I'm under the stone," called the voice. Looking down, Victoria could just see the tip of a leg poking out from underneath a stone. She ran round to the other side, and saw a poor little spider who had two of its eight legs trapped by the stone and could not move.

"How did you get there?" asked Victoria.

"I know it sounds silly," said the spider, "but I came out to make sure that my webs had not been blown away. I was walking along in the shelter of this wall when I was showered with earth and stones. The next thing I knew I was trapped by a stone."

The spider looked very wet and miserable. "I have been calling and calling for hours," she said, "but no one has heard me because everyone is safe and sound inside their homes."

Victoria felt sorry for the spider, but she knew that the stone was too heavy for her to lift on her own, and who would help? As the spider had already discovered, all the woodland creatures were either tucked up in their houses waiting for the rain to stop, or asleep in their dens waiting for the spring.

"There's nothing for it," she decided at last. "I shall have to ask Ben. Benjamin," she called. "Benjamin." Normally, of course, Victoria's tiny fairy voice would never have been heard above the noise of the storm, so she used a fairy code that carried her gentle voice through the rain, over the trees, past the wind right up to the door of Ben's house.

Ben was curled up in bed with the covers pulled over his head so he would not have to listen to the rain. The last thing an elf like Ben wanted to do was to go out into the storm. At first he pretended not to hear Victoria's fairy call, and crawled further under the covers with his hands over his ears. When she called out again, he knew he would have to go and find out what she wanted. He arrived there in a twinkling.

"Well, Victoria Plum," said a very cross and very wet Benjamin, "I hope you've got a good excuse for getting me out of my warm, dry house on a stormy day like this."

"Yes, I have," replied Victoria. "This poor spider is trapped underneath a big stone and I need your special strength to help lift the stone." Victoria knew very well that if she flattered Ben he would soon stop being cross, and when he realised that Victoria could not manage without him he was only too willing to help.

"Leave it to me," said Ben, puffing out his chest to show how strong he was. "I'll soon have her free."

Together they set to work. Ben used all his strength to lift the stone, and Victoria helped with her strongest spell. With Ben puffing and pushing and Victoria chanting the magic words to herself, slowly the stone rolled away and released the spider's legs. Ben took a deep breath, stretched his aching muscles and said, "Right. That's it then. I'm off," and before anyone had a chance to say "elf" he was gone.

"Well, fancy that!" said the spider, very surprised.

"Oh, don't mind him," replied Victoria. "It's just his way." Victoria looked closely at the spider. The two legs which had been trapped were broken and she was clearly in no state to look after herself.

"If you can manage to walk on your six good legs and come into my house," said Victoria, "I have lotions and potions there that will mend the broken ones." The poor spider was very grateful. Slowly and painfully she lifted herself off the ground and, with Victoria's help, she made her way into the house.

"Ah," said the spider, when they were inside, "what a lovely fire." This time the fire had not gone out, so the spider settled herself down in front of the hearth to get warm and dry.

Victoria went into the room at the back of the house where she kept the jars and bottles and books that held all her magic secrets. She wanted very much to cast a spell that would cure the spider in seconds, but she was too young to know how to use the powerful magic of the senior fairies. Instead she would have to use one of her special fairy ointments. It might take a little longer, but at least she knew it would work.

The first thing she did was to open her Magic Recipe Book. She did not want to mix up the wrong ointment, so she followed the recipe exactly: a spoonful of essence of dew, a sprinkling of fairy dust, a pinch of powdered gossamer, and a drop of liquid from a bottle marked "Something Special". When the ingredients were mixed together she smoothed the ointment on to the spider's legs. The spider started to feel better almost at once.

"What we need now are some splints to hold your legs in place while the ointment works," said Victoria. She went into her store and found two pine needles. "They're just the job," she declared, and gently bound them in place.

"I'm afraid it may be uncomfortable for a few days," Victoria told the spider, "but after that you'll be as right as rain."

Something Special

Victoria liked having a guest in the house. She spent much of the time alone during the winter because most of her friends did not like the cold and damp and only came out when it was fine. Sometimes Ben would call and see her and they would sit drinking hot soup and gossiping about all the marvellous times they had together during the lovely warm summer months.

Once a week Victoria flew to the heart of the Great Wood to the house where the old alchemist lived. There she learned about herbs and potions, spells and magic, for the old gnome had once worked with the fairies in the fairy kingdom. Now he was very old, and preferred the peace and quiet of the countryside where he could read his books, discover new magic, and help the junior fairies with their homework. Victoria was very fond of the old man, but she could not visit him every day, so each winter she spent long days walking by herself in the woods, and sitting by the fire reading all her favourite books.

Victoria loved to read. She liked adventure stories and mystery stories, but best of all she liked fairy stories. She would sit for hours reading about the fairy kingdom where all the senior fairies and woodland spirits lived, and about the wonderful magic they did there. Now that Victoria had a friend in the house, she read her books out loud so that the spider could enjoy them as well.

ANCIENT
JUNIOR SPELL BOOK
100
Special Juice
SPELL IN

The stories they both liked best were the ones about Fairy Queen Elena. She had been one of the most beautiful, wisest and cleverest fairies in the kingdom. Her magic was so powerful that when she was Queen the whole world had been a kind and happy place to live. As they came to the end of one story the spider said, "One day, Victoria Plum, you'll be a great and important fairy just like Elena, and people will write stories about you." Victoria blushed and replied shyly, "Oh, no. I've still got so much to learn. I'll never be as good as Queen Elena." The spider just smiled to herself. "Just you wait and see," she said knowingly. Then she closed her eyes and nodded off for her cosy afternoon nap. The spider stayed with Victoria for nearly two weeks. When the time came for Victoria to take off the splints she saw that the ointment had worked perfectly and the two legs were as good as new. Victoria did not want her friend to go. She had enjoyed her company and they had become such good friends, but the spider had a home of her own, and now that she was well again she was anxious to get back. As she said goodbye at the door of the house she told Victoria, "You have been so kind and so generous that if I can ever help you in any way you only have to ask." Victoria said she would, and they both promised to keep in touch and stay good friends for ever.

During the next few weeks the days became colder and colder. Then early one morning Victoria awoke to a gentle swoosh-plop-swoosh-plop noise outside. She hopped out of bed and peeped through the window. The sky was full of the fattest, fluffiest snowflakes she had ever seen. They were tumbling down between the trees and piling up on the ground in soft, white folds.

"Oh, how beautiful," cried Victoria. As she watched, everything in the wood began to change. The dark brown earth became a glittering white carpet. The jagged old tree stump was turned into a fairy castle. The trees that had stood bare and twiggy without their leaves were hung with delicate flowers which blossomed and grew as the snow fell.

By lunchtime the snow had stopped. The clouds blew away and the sun shone out of a clear, blue sky. The sunbeams danced over the snowflakes, making everything sparkle. Victoria decided she had never seen the wood look so pretty. Just then she caught sight of Ben flying through the trees with what looked like a flying carpet.

"Come on, Victoria," he shouted. "I've made a toboggan to play with." He jumped on his toboggan and skimmed down one of the steepest drifts so fast that when he reached the bottom of the slope he disappeared into a deep bank of snow. Victoria heard a giggle from the pile of snow, and saw it wriggle as Ben popped out grinning from ear to ear.

Victoria had never been on a toboggan before and it looked great fun. She pulled on her boots and warm coat, and popped on a snug woolly hat to keep her ears warm. Ben had pulled the toboggan back to the top of the slope.

"Go on," he said. "Climb on and have a go."

Victoria sat on the toboggan, held on tight, and very gingerly began to push herself down the snowy hill.

"Not like that," laughed Ben. "Put some effort into it," and he gave her a mighty push. Off went Victoria with the wind rushing at her face as she slid faster and faster down the steep slope. She was not at all frightened. In fact she enjoyed it so much that when she got to the bottom she could not wait to fly back to the top to have another go.

"My turn now," said Ben, and while Victoria was still brushing the snow out of her hair he raced back to the top ready to slide down the hill again. They were both so busy playing that neither of them noticed the puppy. He came bouncing through the trees, scattering snow in all directions, and almost collided with Victoria and Ben.

"What do you think you're doing?" said Ben. "You frightened the life out of me creeping up like that!" The puppy looked very surprised.

"I didn't creep up on you," he said. "I ran and scampered and tossed snow in the air! I must say, though, snow is funny stuff. It doesn't matter how much you throw it around, it doesn't make any noise."

Victoria had to agree with the puppy. "You're quite right," she said. "Everything in the Great Wood is silent except us," and all three stood quite still for a whole minute just so that they could all listen to the silence. Then all of a sudden Victoria started to giggle. "You do look funny, puppy," she said. "You've got a huge dollop of snow right on the end of your nose."

"So I have," said the puppy, looking down his fat, brown nose until his eyes almost met in the middle. Then he tossed his head so that the big lump of snow flew high up into the air and showered all over Ben and Victoria.

That was the start of the biggest snowball fight there had ever been in the Great Wood! Victoria and Ben pelted each other with snowballs as fast as they could make them, while the puppy dug holes with his podgy little paws, scattering huge sprays of snow over everything within range. Then he pounced on the snow, rolled in it, buried his nose deep inside the biggest drifts, and dug for imaginary snow bones. None of them could remember when they had enjoyed themselves so much.

When all three were quite exhausted and could not think of any more games to play, Ben said he thought it was time he went home to his tea. All that fresh air and exercise had made him hungry. He said goodbye to the puppy and Victoria, and flew off through the trees, taking his toboggan with him.

Victoria and the puppy began to walk home together.

"Thank you for letting me join in your games, Victoria," said the puppy. "I had no idea that snow could be such fun."

"But if you didn't come out to play in the snow," asked Victoria, "why were you racing through the wood?" The puppy looked a little sad.

"I was trying to catch the snowflakes," he replied. "I heard my master say that every snowflake has the most beautiful pictures locked inside. He said they were made from ice, and no matter how many snowflakes fell, each picture was different. It sounded so beautiful that I wanted to see it for myself, but each time I caught a snowflake it disappeared before I had time to see anything at all."

Victoria did not like to see the puppy looking sad, but she knew that delicate snowflakes are one of the most difficult things in the world to catch. Then she had a good idea.

"You wait here," she told the puppy. "I think I know how we can catch a snowflake." Victoria flew off into the wood, and while the puppy was still wondering what she could mean, she was back again, bringing her friend the spider. Victoria had already explained that the puppy wanted to see the snowflakes, so before he could ask any questions, the spider climbed on to a nearby bramble bush. Victoria brushed away the snow so that two of the branches were quite clear, and then the clever spider set to work.

The little puppy was spellbound. He watched as the creature started to spin. Backwards and forwards she went, then round and round as if she was weaving the finest lace. Only minutes later she was finished, and there between the branches was a perfect snowflake net. The puppy whizzed round and round with delight.

"Oh, you are so clever," he said to the spider. "Not at all," she replied. "The fairies always catch the early morning dew in my webs, so why shouldn't we catch snowflakes for a change?" Victoria looked up at the sky. "All we need now," she said, "is some snow." At that moment, as if by fairy magic, the sky was filled with a rush and tumble of snow. As the delicate flakes dropped towards the ground, one was caught for a few seconds on the threads of the spider's web. The puppy peered at it closely. At first he could not make out anything, then he saw the secret pictures he had heard about. There were hundreds of tiny slivers of ice all interlaced to make the most lovely patterns. As one flake melted and disappeared, another was ready to take its place, each one more beautiful than the last. Eventually it stopped snowing and there were no more flakes to catch in the web.

"That was the loveliest thing I have seen," said the puppy. "Each time it snows I will find a snowflake net so I can watch the pictures and remember my friends who showed me the snowflakes' secrets."